The Green of Sunset

The Green Of Sunset

―――――――――

Poems by

John Brantingham

Foreword by Donna Hilbert

November 2013

The Green of Sunset
© Copyright 2013 by John Brantingham
All rights reserved. No part of this book may be used or reproduced in any manner whatsoever without written permission, except in the case of credited epigraphs or brief quotations embedded in articles or reviews.

Editors
Ricki Mandeville
Michael Miller

Graphic design
Michael Wada

Front cover art
Ann Brantingham

Back cover photo
Ann Brantingham

Moon Tide logo design
Ricki Mandeville

The Green of Sunset
is published by
Moon Tide Press
Irvine, California
www.moontidepress.com

Website designed by Mindy Nettifee and John Turi

FIRST EDITION

Printed in the United States of America

ISBN # 978-0-9839651-7-6

For Annie

Contents

Foreword by Donna Hilbert   11

PART ONE

The Green of Sunset	15
The Butterfly Effect	16
Poem to the Child Who Was Almost My Son	18
Thinking about Wilfred Owen	19
Apology to Madeline	21
The Operation, Autumn 1979	22
A Week after the Operation, Autumn 1979	23
The Dog, Autumn 1979	24
A Man Stepping into a River	25
Lightning Storm	26
Prince Toto, Despot of the Ant Nation	28
Building Los Angeles	31
My Little Cactus Blossom	32
Stopping at a Target in New York	33
Stopping for Lunch in Watertown	34
My Second Self	35
Up Here in Rural Canada	36
Five Pins	37
God Save the Queen	38
The Grand Canyon	39
The Wages of Cynicism	40
After 20 Years I Return to London	41
The British Museum	42
Westminster Abbey, March 1991	43
Investigating Turner in the Tate Gallery	44
Café London	45
On a Train from Scotland to London	46
Seems Like I've Been Here Before	47
N. Hollywood No. 3 by Lisa Hight	48
Shane	49
Where We're All Going	50

PART TWO

Parley with the Barbarians	53
As a Boy, I Shoot a Hun	54
Barbarian Magic	55
Brotherhood	56
The God of Lindisfarne	57
The Trail to Bearpaw Meadow, Sequoia National Park, 1978	58
The Trail to Bearpaw Meadow, Sequoia National Park, 1985	59
The Trail to Bearpaw Meadow, Sequoia National Park, 2005	60
Edmonton, Summer 1974	61
Mythology	62
Starbucks on a Saturday Night	63
Meditations on a Lightning Storm that Happened in 1894	64
Summer 1982	65
After the Earthquake	66
Up Towards Weaver Lake	67
Poem about the Pacific Crest Trail that Devolves into a Kind of Sentimentality I'm Not Ashamed Of	68
Sequoia National Park, 1987	69
San Dimas, 1987	70
Afterwards I Stayed Outside for an Hour Before They Made Me Come In	71
Sometimes at Night, It Falls on Me Still	72
I Forgot to Say	73
In Praise of Dogs Who Howl at the Moon	74
The Wind's Will	75
Edgar Degas's *Waiting*	76
The Sound of an Airplane	77
The Art of Merging	78
The Art of Falling	79
The Car Breaks Down on the 99 Up Near Fresno	80
Waking Up on Highway 99	81
Tuesday and You're Feeling Green	82
Sitting in My Father's House on a Summer Afternoon While He Is Away	83
The Late-August Weather Report in Los Angeles	84
Acknowledgments	87
About the Author	88

Foreword

I have looked for it most days since I have known about it: the green of sunset. I have sat on my porch watching as the sun dissolves into ocean. And once, to impress some fellow with my acuity, I said, "There it is, I see it." But, really, I didn't.

I read *The Green of Sunset* straight through, something I seldom do, but it wasn't reading as much as participating in an act of devotion. While I was being entertained, I was also schooled to see, feel, and appreciate this world in a way that I don't always take the time to do.

John Brantingham has seen the improbable flash, the complimentary color, just as he has seen the almost imperceptible glints of gold in the sands of daily life, as he has seen the human faces behind the windshields in the sea of freeway crawlers. He has looked at a sonogram and imagined the life of the child who might have been his own to cherish and guide to manhood. To imagine is to dream behind the curtain of the certain. Brantingham does that. In reading Brantingham, I think of Basho:

> *Deep autumn*
> *my neighbor, how*
> *does he live, I wonder?* (R.H. Blyth tr.)

Brantingham wonders about the lives of others. He would be at home in the company of the haiku masters, making poetry from daily life and making from that poetry devotion. Instead of haiku from the Japan of another era, he has fashioned the prose poems of *The Green of Sunset* from city streets, discount stores, museums; from London, L.A., New York, Canada; from strangers, loved ones, animals and insects—all part of the great cacophony of person and place that is existence. He takes it all in. What is vision then, but paying close attention? And, what is attention if not an act of love?

The Green of Sunset is at its heart a love letter to life itself.

Donna Hilbert
Long Beach, Autumn 2013

Part One

The Green of Sunset

I saw your sonogram this morning, heard your heartbeat for the first time, and it got me thinking about life, how long it is, how much happens to one person. I wished you health and happiness, of course, but thinking about you fifty years from now, I mostly hoped the world would not make you disappointed and bitter. If life does beat you down, I hope you realize bitterness comes only from moments that stick out in our minds like pustules on a tongue. We chew on them, give them an importance they don't have to have, forget that anything else exists. I hope you remember that there are good times too, beautiful times, and more importantly there are all those moments in between the good and the bad. That's what life is, those moments in between—like when a sunset goes from orange to green. People forget the green of sunset because it's not as dramatic as the orange burst at the end of the day or the void of black at the beginning of the evening, but it's there for a second we all ignore. If you find you have become bitter on your fiftieth birthday, I want you to dwell not so much on the great loves and graduations as on the trip to the supermarket when you had a craving for a kiwi fruit or the long walk home from school when you just thought about your day. I hope you remember that there are so many green moments you will have forgotten, as you will most certainly forget what happened today, for these moments inside your mother, these moments you will not be able to remember, are just as important and just as real as any other moment. Today, you danced inside your mother because she drank orange juice. If you ever become bitter, remember that there was a moment today when we all watched you dance your orange juice dance and listened to your orange juice heart and though you cannot remember it, you heard your father's voice through the thin flap of your mother's stomach as he said, "My beautiful child, I love you, I love you, I love you."

The Butterfly Effect

I overhear someone who's describing the butterfly effect, or chaos theory, which is the idea that a butterfly flapping its wings in Kansas begins the chain reaction of events that builds and builds until eventually it starts a typhoon in the South China Sea—one large enough to take out cities, ruin roads, destroy lives, kill people—a typhoon that will require humanitarian aid from countries that are generally China's enemies, one that will bring a re-evaluation of the way we all think of China, even the most nationalistic of us, one that will cause the most religious of us to wonder what God is doing up there and why he chose this particular form of retribution—all of that from the wings of a tiny butterfly sitting on a rose petal in Kansas—and all I can think is why are these doomsday butterflies such goddamn assholes? Hasn't China suffered enough? Aren't the poverty and overpopulation and earthquakes and Maoists and English invaders and Japanese invaders and all the rest they've had to suffer through sufficient cosmic punishment for whatever karmic sin they've committed? Should they really have to put up with butterflies hell-bent on chaos and pain? And come to think of it, haven't we all suffered enough? Isn't there enough intolerance and disease to go around that we don't need chaos insects to fuck everything up even more? I think of Sammy, my child who's coming into the world in a few months, and frankly I don't want him to deal with the doom butterfly of hurricanes or the doom butterfly of pestilence or war or anger or poverty. I don't want him to have to deal with butterflies bent on racism or sexism or dog fighting, and if I were a different kind of man, I would march down to my closest Monsanto wholesaler and write a check for the biggest vat of butterfly insecticide that I could find, and I'd get a giant atomizer that I could put in the back of my truck, and I would drive the back roads of Kansas like a deranged Johnny Appleseed taking out all the fucking doomsday butterflies I could, and I would do it without fear or guilt but only approbation and well-deserved thanks from the entire Chinese nation and from Sammy as well, and when I had run out of the butterfly spray, I would walk the fields of Kansas stamping out any butterfly I happened upon: the butterfly of greed, the butterfly of bad grammar, the butterfly of despair. But that is not who I am, and that's not exactly what I want. What I want is for Sammy to understand that he can kill butterflies. After all, this is his world now, and if I take out all the chaos butterflies, in twenty years, he will face crickets of mass destruction or ladybugs of apathy, and he won't have any idea how to deal with them. What I want is for him to be bitten by the mosquitos of hope and joy and wisdom until their diseases grow inside my son, and he sees how possible it is for him to be the one who can conquer the butterflies of penury and jealousy. I want to watch him become a grown man who corners the chaos butterfly of pointless ancient hatred, wrestles it down to the ground, and pulls out and eats its still beating heart before its quickly fading eyes.

Poem to the Child Who Was Almost My Son

Today I will tell you the stories that I have kept to myself on purpose. I will tell you of the day I hiked the mountain by myself, and I veered off the path and climbed straight up to the crest. There was a clearing in the trees and wild rose bushes growing up in the sun. The afternoon warmth and smell of pine drowsed me, so I lay down and drifted off, only to wake up to nap amnesia and a world of roses before me. And I will tell you about the time I opened the scar on my leg, climbing a fence in the September Santa Ana heat. I sat down in the weeds of a vacant lot and watched the line of red form and drip and pool, and I smiled to see it, but I don't know why, and I didn't know then. I will tell you all the stories that I never meant to tell anyone, the stories that were so precious I kept them hidden. I will tell them to you now because your other father, the man you will always know as father, the man who will give you everything else, cannot give these to you, and I will give them to no one else but you. So I will give you the day when I wandered outside alone at night for the first time in my young life, and I bent my neck back, and I became an astronomer, and I will give you the moment I crushed the bones in my arm in frustration and horror, and I will give you the moment I felt you move inside your mother, and I was sure you would be my son forever.

Thinking about Wilfred Owen

I was thinking about Wilfred Owen today, the poet from World War I who wrote about gas and trenches and the humiliation of fighting in a battle and who died a week before Armistice Day. There was a time in my life when I read everything he wrote and decided to write my Ph.D. dissertation about him before I decided to write about someone else and then someone else and then I dropped out of the Ph.D. I was thinking about him and that time I spent loving his clean description and the beauty of his humanity. I thought of him because a friend was telling me about unmanned drones, the drones that fly raids over Iraq and Afghanistan by people on bases who have remote control of them and how if the person with the controls loses contact with the drone, it is programmed to come back to base. It doesn't self-destruct or crash into the ground. It simply turns around and flies itself over the Mediterranean or old Carthage or wherever it is and through the gentle skies above the Atlantic and lands itself on the runway where it waits patiently for someone to take care of it.

And I suppose I might have made some kind of maudlin declaration about how Owen would have reacted to the drone and the way it works without the need for human interaction, but somehow, I stopped thinking of Wilfred Owen. And I didn't think of the pilot who had lost track of the plane, sighed and shook his head, and went out to the commissary for a cup of coffee and the daily candy bar that he thought of as his own secret treat.

Instead, I thought of the man who must wait on the runway for orders and who had been ordered to take care of the drone when it came back. I thought of him taking the drone into some kind of hangar, and I thought of the care he took of it as he washed it down, the way he used to wash that first car he bought when he was seventeen and had his first real job. I thought of him lost in a dream of how wonderful it was to own that car and how he smiled a little while polishing it, and how we all do that when we're doing little chores. I do that when I'm cleaning up my office and putting away my books, and I think about that Ph.D. I realized I didn't want, and you can bet the man who lost track of the drone dreams as he eats his candy bar. He comes back to that candy bar every day because his mother gave him one when he did something good, and she's gone now, but he still has their ritual. I wonder if Wilfred Owen did something like that on his last day, polishing a rifle and thinking about the little Shropshire house where his girl lived. Maybe she had looked at him shyly while her father called to her. Maybe she moved her fingers in a little wave that only Wilfred could see.

Apology to Madeline

I'm sorry for that night, so sorry about your dress and your necklace, sorry when I think about that mad hour when you wanted to try out our fresh new bodies and I was young and shaky, but I guess not too young, and we had the baseball field, and I'm sorry about afterwards when we sat in the damp grass, and you wept at me, and I said I didn't understand, but I did—I knew that this was the end of everything, and all we had been to ourselves, and I was sorry.

The Operation, Autumn 1979

After the injection, they have me lying on a gurney in the hall outside the operating room, and I can hear a woman gossiping down the hall. She has the same voice as a woman who has a recurring role on a sitcom I watch. I know that, but I can't remember what the sitcom or the role is, and I can't concentrate on the voice enough to hear the words, just her whining drone, up and down, unending, violent in my ears. Later in the operating room, they place the mask over my face and tell me to count backwards, but I've had enough of this world, so instead of counting, I take one breath, as deep as I can, and I hold it as long as I can.

A Week after the Operation, Autumn 1979

I can finally hear again, and the field across the street where the wind blows through the trees in the pulsating *whoosh* of the Santa Ana winds is the only place in the world that makes sense to me, so I sit down in grass and watch a gardener lost in his work across the street. He's chopping at some overgrown weeds in someone's front yard with a blade, and just over the slow rhythm of the wind, I can make out the *thunt, thunt, thunt* of his blade. There's a sweat stain covering his back, but when he straightens out, he's smiling.

The Dog, Autumn 1979

Eight days after the operation, I'm walking home by myself when a dog starts to bark at me from behind his gate. I must have heard a dog before then. I must have. But the sharpness of his yelling fills my ears, and he stops me, and I cannot move from the place I'm standing until someone comes out and finds me staring at him and weeping.

A Man Stepping into a River

A man stepping into a river watches the ripple of his foot dissipate away into the waters, and he thinks about all those poems and songs that talk about impermanence, and he is tempted for a moment to become maudlin and existential about the way time washes away everything, but the truth is that his foot did make an impression, his print was there, and just for a second, even running water was perfectly etched in his image and showed that he existed, that he was there, that he had done something.

Lightning Storm

I'm teaching class during a storm that's happening at the exact same time a solar flare is arcing off the sun on an afternoon when four planets plus Pluto are aligned, and I'm into a long discussion of metaphysics when I sneeze just as a lightning bolt passes over my head, stretching all the way to my house three miles away, and in that moment back at home my dog sneezes, and for a moment, my soul is taken out of my body, and Archie's soul is taken out of his body, and we switch bodies, and for a brief time, Archie gains human consciousness, and I gain dog consciousness, and we both start to bark.

For in that one moment, Archie can see his whole life so far stretching behind him, and he sees a clock, and he gains that human understanding of what time is, and that he's had time and that time is moving ahead of him, but that time is something that comes and disappears, and that time is going to come and disappear, and that he's heading for something that smells a lot like the end of his time, and that he's going to end some day, that he's going to die—just fucking die—and he's never spoken English before, so he starts to bark at my students—he loses it and starts barking through my body, trying to make the words that tell them he wants to do something—he has to accomplish something—it all has to mean something in some kind of profound way and aside from taking nice walks and guarding my house from well-intentioned neighbors—he can't see that he's done all that much even though I keep telling him he's a good boy.

He barks existentially about time and the past and his puppyhood and he barks religiously wondering if there's a dog god and if all dogs truly do go to heaven, and he barks about all the wasted time, time we could have been together, but we were filling up hours with chores and arguments and worries, and he barks about politics and the Sudan and health care and the state of the government and how Pluto is no longer a planet and the fact that we're laying off teachers and the Invisible Children and the fact that we've let all of this become so overwhelming in our heads that we push it all out.

He barks about all of this and more until he's just barking and barking and then those barks turn into a scream, a long howling scream that makes my students wonder what all of this means and how it relates to the class, and the scream turns into a realization that he can speak English, and he wants all the answers and maybe some of these wide-eyed young people have the answers, when he sneezes again and finds himself back in his body, and I find myself back in my body, my voice now hoarse from barking and screaming.

But Archie can still see it all. He understands it all from a human point of view and a dog point of view and he keeps on barking, keeps on trying to speak to my wife, who is in the living room on her haunches trying to tell him that it's just lightning and thunder, and that he's all right, but he can't take it so he goes into the backyard and tilts his head upwards calling out to Pluto, letting all the dogs on Pluto know that he knows and he feels and he wishes they could have a planet instead of whatever it is that Pluto has become but that sometimes we don't get anything that we wanted—sometimes we just get that dash of knowledge that ruins the whole thing. He barks all of this at the sky until he is howling so loudly my wife can't tell the thunder from his barks anymore.

Prince Toto, Despot of the Ant Nation

You're on your motorcycle on a freeway overpass that crosses the L.A. River when you get sick of the guy ahead of you in the blue Hyundai with the big dent that's smashed in his right rear tail light, the guy who's going 50 miles an hour in a 65 zone, and though you know you're not supposed to, you pass him on his right. It's a stupid move, but one you've made safely 10,000 times (always swearing about people who drive slowly in the left lane) except this time, this one time, he moves right with you, no signal (how could he, the tail light's been bashed in) and no easing over, just a quick cut into your lane before you can react, before you can brake, before you can swerve. He comes into your lane and knocks into the side of your motorcycle, just a tap, but it's enough, and before you know it, you find yourself separated from your bike, separated from the bridge that's curving, sailing now out over the side with only the mostly empty L.A. River, empty except for that blue deep part that runs right down the middle of it, out into what (you have to admit to yourself) is probably the last few moments of your life, and you look back at the driver who's looking back at you and rolling his eyes as if to say that anyone who tries to pass on the right in L.A. traffic deserves what he gets.

Also, the driver in the blue Hyundai has a pencil moustache. He might be French.

It is at this moment that your brain takes over, and you flash through your life stopping for some unknown reason at a moment during that year when you tutored at that English as a Second Language school, and you worked closely with that older guy from Vietnam, who you kind of hated in secret, but you couldn't say anything because he'd been through so much. He'd lived through the reeducation camps, had been tortured, had survived, and had taken a boat across the Pacific for a new life and amnesty. He'd been through all that so you couldn't say anything, but he always sneered at you, and one day he told you that there was no way you could have ever lived through the prison camps, that you were weak, and the guards would have recognized your weakness, and they would have shot you on the first day because you weren't going to survive anyway, but you could at least be useful to them as an example. You told the old Vietnamese man that you really just wanted to get through the lesson on how to conjugate the verb "to spank," and he sneered and went back to telling you how pathetic you were.

It was at this moment that you happened to notice a dead cricket on the ground surrounded by ants, and you retreated into a daydream. You had dreamed that the cricket was named Prince Toto, that he had been an average sort of cricket until he realized that he would only be a regular cricket among other crickets, but he could easily enough enslave an ant population, who were (let's face it) willing to be workers already. Prince Toto set up shop outside the local ant colony, making all the ants praise him for his handsomeness, taking young ant virgins for his concubines, making ants fight to the death with broken bottle shards. As the old Vietnamese guy berated you, you descended deeper and deeper into the daydream until you hated Prince Toto, hated him body and soul. You hated his stupid cricket sneer, and the way he smelled after he had defiled a new virgin ant. You hated everything about him, and you hated him when you went home that night and just tried to have a nice meatloaf in peace, but it was hard to eat well with all that hate, and the world full of unjust crickets, and you kind of hated that old Vietnamese guy for making you dream of Prince Toto.

And it occurs to you, sailing over the L.A. River, that there is a good chance that all that time you spent hating Prince Toto was wasted time. It occurs to you that Prince Toto, being a figment of your imagination, probably never lost any sleep because of your hatred, and any anxiety you had was all yours, you wasted the whole evening and a perfectly good meatloaf, and that your life would have been a lot easier and a lot better if you had just loved him. Maybe your love for him could have transformed him. Sure, he had an ant fetish, but maybe he would have settled down with a nice ant woman instead of raping all those poor ant girls. Your love could have changed him, could have made him better.

And it occurs to you that maybe you should have loved that old Vietnamese guy. The truth was that he was never going to get the verb forms down, and unless he had his own fetish he wouldn't really need to conjugate the verb "to spank," and the best thing for him was just to speak to someone in English, which is what he was doing. He was a bore, but he'd kind of earned it after all.

And it occurs to you right now, sailing through the air in your last moment, that you should have been loving a lot of people, that love is a skill that must be practiced like any skill until you have it down just right, that loving people is a full-time occupation, and you cannot just love your family and the people who do nice things to you but everyone, even the French pencil-mustachioed man in the blue Hyundai who has begun to shake his head in disgust. Even him you have to love.

And it occurs to you that this is a pretty big revelation. This is your moment, and it would be kind of sad if it all ends, you dead on the concrete side of the L.A. River, next to your motorcycle. There's only one chance that you can see, and you hope that the French pencil-mustachioed man tapped you just right, and that you were going at just the right speed, and that everything is working out just perfectly so that you will land in the water in the deep middle part of the L.A. River.

You hope that you live long enough to bring this message of love to all of L.A., and that you begin to love all people—especially French pencil-mustachioed maniac drivers, especially angry old abusive Vietnamese men, especially Prince Toto, despot of the ant nation.

Building Los Angeles

Building a city is the most unconscious of all arts. A place like L.A. is brought together by love, by hate, by compromise. L.A. was built by millions of artists, separate spaces that became communal life, hiding what shamed us, pushing forward what defined us. It takes a resident to know it all, about the water we pump in and the runoff that drains in concrete rivers to the sea, about the fires and earthquakes, the kids living on ketchup and mustard, the crime, the graffiti that says "I was here" and "I matter" and sometimes "Watch out," the bomb shelters from our last age still lying underground, the politics, the poverty, the wealth. You see none of that as you buzz through the city. Instead, as you drive down the I-5 at ten o'clock in your rented convertible on a warm summer night, you come up over a rise and see the snaking headlights wending through a bed of streetlights a hundred miles wide, and just when you thought you realized why everyone stays, they start the fireworks over Disneyland and you can just hear everyone in the cars rumbling beside you say, "Aaaaah!"

My Little Cactus Blossom

So I'm up in the mountains above L.A., hiking through the scrub that's not burning this fall, and I step straight into a cactus, cutting up my ankles, getting stuck a thousand times, and in my thrashing around, I kick off one of the blossoms.

Weeks later (while I'm still recovering) the rains come and wash away all the debris, scat, and little bits of paper left by hikers and my cactus blossom too, of course, and all of it rushes down the side of the hill in a muddy mess down into the city and into the concrete river. It's the river that flows right into the suburbs, into water shimmering with suburban oil, and my blossom's there too with the bottle some homeless guy used to stay warm when the rains started and straws dropped in someone's backyard from a McDonald's celebration after a school play. And it bobs along the now swollen drainage, knocking into leftover ingredients for meatloaf and pho and tamales and barbeque, spurred on through the neighborhoods by the music of Brazil and Germany and Mexico and China and America too, of course.

When it finally gets into the actual city, it flows down beneath bridges, the kind you see in movies and you say, "Yeah, that's L.A.," and it goes past those old neo-classical buildings that you see in all the old film noir flicks. It bobs along until it's riding parallel to the Alameda Corridor with all those people holding it all together when everything inside them is screaming, holding it all together even though the rain is showering smog back down on them, holding it all together for the sake of whoever is waiting at the end of the drive.

It goes out to Long Beach, past people fishing in the dirtiest water in the world, just so they can throw whatever they catch back in and tell someone what they caught even though every once in a while, someone reels in a body. It bobs out into the Long Beach Harbor, out where the rich people take their boats on nicer days than this. It gets caught by some undercurrent and goes out of the harbor, out out out out maybe out towards Hawaii or Alaska or China.

When it gets way out there in the clean ocean, out where it resembles a blossom again, out where there isn't sludge and waste and whatever else is floating around L.A., I give it a thought, and the thing is, I feel a little sorry for it now.

Stopping at a Target in New York

The Targets in upstate New York are no different than the Targets in Los Angeles. They are the same nationwide: 3000 miles of conformity and comfort. And where you would find toilet paper in a beautiful quilted stack in Nashville, you will find that same stack in Seattle. The music is the same, the coffee is the same, and the same people stock shelves and smile at you from behind their red vests. It's no surprise that coming into this Target with Anders, I run into myself, the me that would have been if I had not moved to California when I was a kid. We're both there, me and my other self—me with Anders—my other self with those kids who would have been mine, a boy and a girl who are dumpy and not too bright, but who he loves in his own way. This is his life, these children he brings in here on a weekday afternoon looking for whatever tennis shoes he can afford. He's become vague, whether it is from his home life or his job, teaching at a high school or working with the forestry service, coming home to his wife who's not quite sure she loves him but becomes suddenly terrified when she imagines him leaving her. He sees me and knows me, and he aches instantly for the life that I have, middle-class, childless, with a woman that I love and a job that I love in a city that I tolerate. I look at him and his kids and think, that would have been all right, and I believe it for a while. It's no surprise, though, that we envy each other a little, I not satisfied with what I have here in this universe and he not satisfied in that universe—all of us disappointed in the possible universes that together we inhabit.

Stopping for Lunch in Watertown

Anders and I pull over for lunch at a diner in upstate New York, a locals' place that probably doesn't get much in the way of tourists since it's off the Interstate and not part of a chain. They're impressed here that I'm from California; it probably fuels dreams of beach cities and movie icons. They're probably thinking of sports cars and rock stars and so many things that they've seen on television, dreams that couldn't be farther from the truth of the suburbs that I've always lived in. They talk to me for a couple of minutes and then go back to their conversation. There are five of them here, all pushing middle age, all grown thick, all losing their hair. They've probably sat here all their lives in that same conversation. I've spent my life bouncing around L.A. and other cities, never feeling rooted to any one place, never growing truly close to any one friend—casual friendships that can and do end—and the people I never see again don't miss me all that much. It would have been different, though, if I had lived here my whole life, for them and me. Maybe it would have been better if I had learned to accept people with their faults, even learned to like them because of their faults. I could have been a better person for knowing these people, but there is no time now. There never has been, and when we're done eating, Anders and I pick up and leave that little diner forever.

My Second Self

I could have easily enough grown up in one of these little towns in Upstate New York—Watertown, Plattsburgh, or Albany, someplace like that—except my father's company sent him west to Los Angeles, and instead of feeling trapped my whole life the way that so many people here do, I've felt uprooted. I suppose it doesn't make much difference, but I'm thinking these kinds of thoughts as Anders and I cross into Canada. Knowing me, he tells me not to joke with the guard, but one glance at the serious young man, and I know I wouldn't have. I can see his whole life written in his face, the life that Exley wrote so well about up here, the life I would have had if we hadn't been put on the other side of the country. There would be long work days and evenings with the kids and a wife, weekends around town watching the kids lose at baseball and half believing the priest at St. Whatever and the whole veneer of a life that I would say that I wanted—that it was just what I wanted—and the booze that would wash over me in the evening would make me believe all that, and I would ignore the dissatisfaction. I know this would be my life because it was the life of uncles and aunts, and, I suppose, eight generations of Brantinghams right back to George who left his dissatisfaction in the little English town named for our family. I can see that all in the guard's face, and so no, I don't make a joke, and I wouldn't have, and sure, I'd be happy to answer any question he has without resentment, without anger over the intrusion, with the love one can show only to one's other self.

Up Here in Rural Canada

Anders is probably the first poet I've ever known who distrusts academia and teachers and schools and education in general. So many of the poets I've brought to the college where I teach are professors themselves. The rest wish they were—all of them except Anders. He tells me as we drive towards his home that he likes his son's current teacher because she doesn't assign homework, and Dan has time to focus on his soccer. He tells me that he advises kids in the area to get a trade. He tells me about why he didn't finish high school, about the physics teacher who belittled him in front of his friends. He tells me about how when I was in college, he was bumming his way through Europe, Asia, India, Africa, and South America. I teach, of course, but I'm no zealot. Why would he trust such a place? He's like so many of the students I've seen, feeling like outsiders, being told that they don't belong. And it's clear to me that (in the parlance of education) he's a kinesthetic learner, someone who thinks most clearly when moving and doing, and there are so few opportunities in class for that kind of kid. Besides, out here in the country, what would he do with an English literature degree? What could someone like me teach him about poetry that he hasn't learned already? So I listen to him and when we get to his house, I don't tell his kids that they should go to college. If they have a passion, they'll do what they want. The rest of that afternoon, when we might have talked about Kooser or Woloch or Locklin, we talk sports and watch Dan kick ball after ball into the goal that Anders has painted on his garage wall. And after all, there is poetry to the curving arc of that boy's kick as well.

Five Pins

We've been driving back and forth through Eastern Canada all day, and Anders' kids have been good, so we pull over to play five pins with them, a variation of bowling I've never seen. It's played with a ball a little larger than a softball, and as the name suggests, you knock over five pins rather than ten. With its smaller balls and no gutters, it's made for kids, clearly, but Anders and I play against his son and daughter to keep them entertained, and for a while, Anders and I vie for the win with Amelia just glad to be there. When Dan realizes how far back he's fallen, something clicks inside him, and he turns into a competitor on the level of Mickey Mantle or Michael Jordan. He is concentration. Between frames, he eyes everyone's style, evaluating weaknesses, gaining advantages. When it's his turn, he makes miracle shots, using physics and geometrical measurements that I'm not sure existed before this moment. In the end, he edges everyone out and the angelic expression of relief that takes over his face is a joy to us all, but it's not a surprise. Competition is this boy's all. It's his passion. It's his love. A person cannot change his passion—he cannot hide it or hide from it. For Anders, it's his family. For me, it's Annie and our life together. But for Amelia, smiling at her brother benevolently, intelligent and sincere beyond her years, simply happy to love her little family, I'm not sure. I think that—like so many of us—she is still looking, and like so many of us she might go on looking her whole life, happy in herself until that passion takes her away.

God Save the Queen

Halfway through a week of giving readings up here in tiny Canadian towns, my buddy Anders sets me up with a reading in a VFW hall. Knowing me, he tells me that there will be a picture of Queen Elizabeth on the stage behind me and that whatever I do, I should not, under any circumstances, make fun of her or make any joke whatsoever. And it's a good thing that Anders knows me that well, because the moment I'm on stage with poor Liz looking at me with those sad eyes that have lived through world wars and divorces and tragedies and depression and anarchy and the complete change of her culture, the moment I see all of that in her tightly closed lips, I almost turn around and go on a rant that starts with me being glad that my forebear got off that foggy little island and ends with me questioning her gender. Of course, none of it would be serious—I have nothing but respect for the old woman who did so much. And turning around to see the faces in the VFW, I am so glad Anders told me what to do. I am surrounded by people who lived through those wars and divorces and tragedies and depression and anarchy with her. I am surrounded by people who believed enough in her to sacrifice money and time and personal goals, and they did it all because she asked, and because she suffered quietly with them and for them. So I do not make fun of her or these people. I show the reverence that she and they so richly deserve, and from now on I will say "God Save the Queen" and "God Save her People" and "God Save Canada" and "God Save All of Us" who need a queen, who would like a queen, who would feel just that much more secure in ourselves and what we were doing if she would step to the edge of her balcony, wave that little wave, and let us know that we were all in this mad, chaotic gumbo together.

The Grand Canyon

Ann heard that there's snow along the rim of the canyon this weekend, so we make a little impromptu foray into Arizona to see this place differently than most people do, and the beauty of it is unspeakable. Just a rime covering the edges, outlining every red rock in silver. Every bush shines. We've brought the dogs, Christina and Archie, even though Christina hobbles everywhere she goes now. She's an old cocker spaniel, an ancient lady who I still think of as a puppy, and I'm already feeling nostalgic about this friend I've known for over a decade. I do that a lot—I always have. I mourn for things before they've gone. I spend the last week of summer vacation worried about how my classes will go, I ruin Sundays thinking about Mondays, which will be fine anyway, and I've spent hours worrying about my own death. It's strange that I should be missing Christina while she's standing here in front of me, and while I'm being tragic about her, I'm missing the fun she's having along the rim, and it seems to me that mourning my own death makes about as much sense as mourning the loss of the Grand Canyon. It's no more permanent than I am, and it will be gone soon enough too. The walls will crumble into the Colorado River below, the earth will shift, and what was once a desert canyon will become savannah or forest or who knows what. We're all dying. We're all going away, Christina, the canyon, and I, but right now, right at this moment, I tell myself, we're all in the middle of the great state of Arizona, all vital, and all beautiful.

The Wages of Cynicism

Imagine me, cynic that I was, 19 years old, sneering at a Yugoslavian village whose favorite daughters and sons talked directly to Mary—the gut reaction of a clever kid—who would, in the next few days, see himself for what he was and learn to hate that fraud inside himself. It's taken me these last twenty years to forgive myself for that, and God, so much more, and it makes me wonder how long it will take for me to forgive myself for all that I am doing today.

After 20 Years I Return to London

And although the town has changed, inside I feel the same. I'm still the same kid who came here feeling stupid and uncouth, the same kid who wanted art and travel, who tried to change himself completely, and even though I return here, having done so much of what I wanted to do, I feel like such an outsider still—so less dashing than everyone else here on the tube heading out from Heathrow—the business men in their trim suits making eyes at the women who keep their own eyes on their magazines. Every kid, every adult seems to share that secret knowledge of how to be cool.

The British Museum

I'm talking to a man in a brown suit in the British Museum about an original Hokusai on loan from Japan, and when he catches my accent, he asks me where I'm from.

"Los Angeles," I say in Californian.

"Los Angeles?" he asks, and he sighs out his West Coast dreams, dreams of sunshine and wealth and convertibles filled with women who help him to forget his discontent. His L.A. is a place of eternal summer where no one is caught up in the frustrating cycle of regret and loss. Everyone there feels joy, has the freedom to pursue passions and impulses, and doesn't have to deal with the intolerance and slow thinking that has kept him trapped in his mean little world of ambiguities and snagging little comments that he has to analyze to understand.

His Los Angeles is my London, and we're standing here in front of Hokusai, looking into a beautiful Japanese past, one of drama and nature, and of course, what we miss is that Hokusai was painting a wave that capsized fishing boats, that destroyed crops, that flooded Japan.

Westminster Abbey, March 1991

I got my first migraine staring at Chaucer's grave in Westminster Abbey. It was a real migraine, complete with an aura that nearly blinded me, and I had nausea and all the rest. I was twenty and living away from home for the first time, and the migraine probably had to do with too much excitement, too much beer and too little water, or a food allergy, or I don't know what, but I didn't know what a migraine was then, so I thought I was having a spiritual moment with old Geoffrey—that he was communing with me, and it felt significant. It seems ridiculous now thinking back, but it made a sort of sense at the time. Life was different in those months. Everything was different. I had fallen in love and found the British reading room and met people from all over—people who had done things like scampering over the Berlin Wall or hitchhiking across Asia—and every night we drank and talked and read and lived. There are times in life when you read the right book at just the right time or meet the right person who understands you or travel some place that silences you for one long lost breath, and you get it, and you understand for the first time, and all of those things were happening to me, all of those celestial events were going on for me in London right then. It was that moment that I got my first migraine, so maybe it's not so strange that I felt like Chaucer was reaching out to me from wherever he was and blessing me and telling me that what I was doing right now was in some way sacred.

Investigating Turner in the Tate Gallery

Halfway through our travels to London, I take my students to the Tate Gallery. We've been to the Tate Modern already where they were introduced to the shock of the modern, but I'm not sure they really saw any of it. They stood there in front of vertical shafts of light or images of bleeding sheep or urinals attached to the wall and called art, and they watched all of it with a silence that noted what I thought was bewilderment or frustration. But now they're in front of Turner's work—all that light and ocean—and they've come to life. They point at it and say things and turn to each other and nod in understanding, and I suppose I could say that their tastes are old-fashioned, even pedestrian, but that's not it. I know because when I was their age, I came to London too, and one cold March evening, I found myself, twenty years old and alone in the big city, standing in front of an original copy of "Kubla Khan" and recognizing it and going to the next case which held "Mutability" and recognizing that and strolling from case to case seeing and understanding whatever I saw and coming to the realization that I was not the idiot that I'd always assumed myself to be—that I'd always been told in so many ways that I was. And this, I know today, is what is happening to so many of my students right now in front of Turner. They're not seeing Turner and his art so much as they're beginning to see themselves. For the first time in their lives, they're seeing themselves not as they've been told to see themselves, but as they actually are, and they're coming awake—before me and that incredible Mr. Turner and themselves—to their true selves, full of unlimited joy, intelligence, and beauty.

Café London

I'm sitting in a café in downtown London in Russell Square next to the British Museum next to the University of London next to the hotel where I'm staying near the tube stop that can take me by train to Paris and from there to Rome or Florence or the Hague or Copenhagen or wherever I want to go. I'm sitting in a café in one of the most sophisticated places in the world wearing my reading glasses, which I only sort of barely need, but I like them because they make me look like an oversized F. Scott Fitzgerald except that you never see him with a beard, and also, I don't think he wore glasses. They cost me ten dollars at a drug store in Walnut, California, but in my mind they look like the accessory of one of the great dons of the university I'm sitting next to or the docents of the museum I can see from my table. I'm wearing a tweed jacket too, something I bought at Goodwill and that cost me less than the glasses. Someone more sophisticated than I am smoked a pipe in it before I owned it—giving me the air of the kind of man who knows his pipe weed and wears tweed jackets and needs to wear tweed jackets because he lives some place like London and says clever things to clever people all day long, people who work at the BBC or the queen's palace or one of those places that when you ask them where they work they say something like "the Institute for Cultural and Gender Studies in a Post-Marxist Age," and you smile and say "a-ha" like you actually know where they work and understand what "Post-Marxist" is but the whole time you're wondering if that means they're really communists. I'm hoping my Goodwill jacket and my drug store glasses make me look like one of those guys when I notice a man staring at me. He's ordering at the counter with his English accent, and I look him over quickly and see that despite the cold, he's wearing flowered Bermuda shorts and flip flops and Ray-Ban knock-off sunglasses and a t-shirt that says "I heart L.A.," and when we lock eyes, I know what both of us will be doing for the next half hour, and although we'll be dreaming of different places, they will be the same place actually, just as real, just as hopeful, just as beautiful.

On a Train from Scotland to London

We're an hour into the trip when I realize that somewhere out there is the little town of Brantingham, the town named after some of my distant forebears, who mostly died in the black plague, whose descendants, my ancestors, were driven out of the area because of their religion, so the family stories go, who rose to fame either through treachery or merit, but called it God's will the way that all the nobility do, who had come to this country in 1066 during the invasion and took it from the poor blond people who lived here. Somewhere out my window are people I share blood with, people who look like me vaguely around the eyes, who share my taste in food, who share my inability to lose weight. And if there is such a thing as genetic memory, I don't have it, and I don't feel comfortable here, and in fact it seems to me that the people on this train don't fully trust me and have been giving me furtive angry glances, and their hatred might just be because of my American accent or perhaps it's all in my head, but I don't feel at home here at all, and it seems to me that my people lived here and owned these lands and ruled these lands and made life generally disagreeable for the people they had conquered and for each other for years. My people lived only miles from Nottingham, after all, and the scabby rich nobles Robin Hood robbed were almost certainly my ancestors. And when I read *Ivanhoe*, I have no illusions about what side my forebears were on. It could be that all of the people who bore my name 900 years ago were kind, gentle souls who used their power gracefully, but my guess is that power corrupts everyone, and my guess is that my people were powerful, and my guess is that if genetic memory exists the people on this train who keep narrowing their English eyes at me are remembering ancient Brantinghams who looked like me, who laughed like me, who took their lands and ruined their lives. If genetic memory exists, then the land must have memory as well, and it is saying a prayer today, that the Brantingham passing across its face will keep moving south to London until he comes to Heathrow and he will take an airplane across the Atlantic to where we have all been driven, where we have lost our nobility—where, I hope, we have finally become kind, gentle souls.

Seems Like I've Been Here Before

In the 1970s, it seemed like everyone on television claimed to be reincarnated, and moreover that everyone who'd come back had been Magellan or Alexander the Great in the last life—someone like that. Actors, politicians, and generals wanted to have been great, to have been remembered because no one wanted to imagine being a milk maid or a beggar even though chances of a simple life were much higher than celebrity.

I've never believed in reincarnation, never thought I was anyone but me, but if it's true, and we're coming back again and again, I hope, in my past life, I wasn't Napoleon or any of his generals. I hope I was a soldier, forced to be in a war I didn't understand and didn't want. I hope I came from a tiny country forgotten now but facing down the Napoleonic war machine, and that I was killed brutally, run through with a bayonet.

I hope as I lay there, I thought about the pointlessness of my sacrifice and the loss of my culture while in my last moments I watched French soldiers destroying what I had known as home, and I hope the pain of that moment reverberates now in my life and stays with me in all my future lives, and that all my future selves understand loss and pain, and that I practice compassion for as many lives as I have before me.

And I hope that as a young man, I saw you, my darling, and I fell in love at once, and I dreamed of you, so that as I lay dying I thought of what a joy it would be to be with you, and I wished that I could spend a lifetime giving you every bit of love I have. What I hope is that in my forgotten little battlefield in my forgotten little country, I thought of you, and that thought reverberates through me now and always will.

N. Hollywood No. 3 by Lisa Hight

And behind the woman in the wedding dress is your whole life, everything you have ever known, everything that Los Angeles has been to you sitting there in the reflection of the store window. All that you are and have been, all the long Santa Ana wind days of your life, all the strip mall love affairs and traffic—all that lies behind her is a blessing upon your life. Bless her then and the world that is reflected around her. Give her blessings for her wedding, blessings for the man who will cut you off on that street, blessing for the woman who will fall out of love with her husband and children in that market. Bless the iron cage behind the window and the shop owner who sees evil everywhere he looks and thinks he needs an iron gate and bless the man who would smash the window and take his vodka except that the gate is there. Bless the wind that whips around her head and makes her dream of the man she wanted to marry, the man she will never marry, the man who sits alone across town thinking of her. Bless the children she will have and the memories she will have of today. Bless her loneliness and your loneliness and the loneliness that exists in all of us who walk down a sidewalk in North Hollywood and watch our lives pulsing away in the reflection in a glass pane.

Shane

When we were fourteen, we thought we were so clever when we named our penises, and come to think of it, we were clever too, in the way boys that age are, crude and naïve all at once. We came up with the usual monikers, Harry Reasoner, Dick Thrust, Sir Martin Wagstaff. And mine? I can't tell you what I named mine. I can't remember anymore except I remember the joy I had saying the name over and over, the joy I had when the other boys heard the name and admired me for it and laughed as well. We were obsessed with the penis as anyone with new testosterone is, but now, of course, I have grown used to it, and I have lost much of it, and my obsessions lie elsewhere. So in the spirit of that boy, I will give names to the body parts that call to me today. I will call my knees Westside Story for the way they snap and click. My colon will be Beowulf while my stomach will be Grendel, for they are locked in a mortal battle. And my hair? My hair will be Shane, Shane who has been shot, Shane who is slowly going away, Shane who only wants to die off screen and out of my sight. "Shane? Shane? Come back, Shane, come back!"

Where We're All Going

In the evenings, we're all going home, each one of us on the 10 freeway, thousands of us, tens of thousands, perhaps millions if you think of how the 10 stretches from Los Angeles to Jacksonville. It doesn't seem possible when you're in the left lane. They all flash so quickly going the other direction—a man thinking about suicide, a pregnant woman who doesn't know about her child, someone worried about taxes, another who knows he'll be in prison in a week, the family who's stopped speaking to each other, the priest who's just been ordained—each passes you in a breath, and the weight of the passion of the world is there, and there's you, driving a little too fast, trying to get back to your lovely wife and contemplating how small you are and how big the world feels and how much pain and joy there is out there, and how most of the time all you want out of the big game is just to get home which is where we're all going together.

Part Two

Parley with the Barbarians

Summer mornings, before it would get too hot to move, we'd ride out to the hills nearby and push our bikes up the streets where the rich kids lived, push them as far as we could and then one by one in a line, coast them downhill in the sprawling California heat.

I'd read something about horsemen on the steppes, had seen an illustration in a textbook once. On the straightaways, I'd raise my arms out from my sides, straighten my spine and shriek my challenge to any who might come.

We'd do that again and again, up and down until sweat slicked our naked chests, and then we'd go to the school yard, five or six of us to play tackle football in the shade of the four great sentinel trees—the trunks our most dangerous blockers.

We, all of us, were barbarians then, but every ten-year-old boy worth his bicycle is. Every one of us dreamed of horsemen and Conan and the promises made to men by drawings in books.

As a Boy, I Shoot a Hun

At ten years old, boys dream of battle. We did anyway, men with swords slipping through the woods, surprising their victims from behind with the strokes that end it all.

We dreamed of Strider and the man with no name and Han Solo, and then one Sunday afternoon, channel five's Family Film Festival played all those ancient versions of *Beau Geste,* and we began to dream of the Foreign Legion and Viking funerals all at once.

And there were knights, of course, always knights—knights jousting and defending and going to strange lands to kill people who disagreed with them, and on the dodge ball court, you could tell which boys might have been knights seven hundred years ago by the way they jumped away from the ball or else stood to catch the thing coming at them.

We were wise enough then to love knights as we hated Nazis, to know that Vietnam had been a tie, just as we'd really won the War of 1812. On the grassy field, after a game of football, all you had to do was mention communists, and we'd all work up enough anger and resentment to have the energy for another game.

It was easy to hate then, easy to imagine my rifle scope rising until I saw a blue-eyed Hun across the field, easy to know what that little kick of power would be when I pulled my trigger, easy to smile at the tiny red cloud that would appear above his head just as he began his last drooping fall to earth.

Barbarian Magic

The first Europeans to see polar bears were Norwegians in 1619, who shot and ate the bears and died soon after (most of them) from eating undercooked bear meat.

Those who lived and came back told stories of giant white monsters roaming vast lands of snow where they'd pilot icebergs and eat people, and these stories mingled in the way that stories did back then with tales of Bigfoot and witches and barbarian magic until the world of Salem, Massachusetts must have seemed held only by providence in the hand of God who was willing to let go on a whim.

This, of course, all according to Wikipedia, which is as good a source as any in a lot of ways, and a better source than anyone in Salem had and will thresh the magic out of any number of things in the same way college draws childhood out of a person like a poison, the way that zoos replaced our terror dreams of the great white hunters of the North and instead made them cute.

Brotherhood

This winter the rains came in hard enough to draw out ancient barbed wire from the forest, like a splinter out of a boy's hand. I take a short cut off the trail, scrambling up the far bank of a creek, and it grabs onto my ankle.

And though I don't know it, it was laid there 103 years ago by a man who forested this land, harvested the trees and let his cattle tromp the mountainside.

When he put it down, he cut himself on a barb, left a little blood. As I free myself, I cut myself on that barb too. I don't know it, but our blood mingles, and he and I become blood brothers, just as I don't know that I have become air brothers with so many people on this mountain, and so many down in town, just as I don't know that I have entered into the brotherhood of molecules and atoms with people and dogs and trees and coyotes and even birds.

All of this I do not know, and I will never find out, and the knowing isn't the part that matters anyway.

The God of Lindisfarne

Back in 1993, my wife painted an illuminated manuscript copy of the Lindisfarne Gospels, pouring her art and her love into it the way that those monks did 1300 years earlier, except that maybe the monks had love of their god on top of that.

Maybe not—there's no way to tell from here whether they were faithful to God or art or a little of both, or whether it felt like the end of the world—like God was giving up on all that was good when the barbarians began to raid.

This place must have seemed to them the one place in the world where art and culture survived, and the Vikings came through stealing and tromping and murdering and raping and that must have felt like the end of everything—the way that so many moments in our lives feel like the end of everything—9/11 and cancer and the loss of your kids and everything is just leaving you and all you have left is that art and then the Vikings take that too—the way that time and mildew took away her manuscript page, the way that time and mildew will pull her and me apart, the way that time and mildew will make us forget even the Vikings, even the monks, even God.

The Trail to Bearpaw Meadow, Sequoia National Park, 1978

The rhythm of my parents' footsteps and conversation dreams me into my own world as I follow them first by three feet and then by seven. Finally, I stop on the trail to hear what it's like to listen to their conversation disappear into the trees as they thread their way on.

The Trail to Bearpaw Meadow, Sequoia National Park, 1985

Summer pushes the scent out of the pines and soon, I find myself stumbling along the trail. At a creek I veer off the trail and uphill until I lie down on a great granite face. I wake up to the whooshing of a warm breeze through ferns. Nearby a coyote grooms himself, but we haven't seen each other yet.

The Trail to Bearpaw Meadow, Sequoia National Park, 2005

The rhythm of footsteps and a conversation wake me out of my walking dream, and I can hear a group threading its way through the trees towards me. I could walk uphill to let them by and stay in the bubble of my world. Instead I pause and step off the trail. When they pass by, I smile and talk to them in the same way I do when I love people.

Edmonton, Summer 1974

And there was my mother, taking deep breaths, cupping her hands and shouting—a sound that lost itself somewhere ten or twelve feet in front of her, my mother, a giant at 4 foot 11, and me at the back of the yard, out there with the blackberry bushes, those bushes I'd tangle myself into to gnaw fruit and bark and thorns, my mother trying to yell over thunder and blowing, the lightning strobing the clouds just above.

In two days, she'd take me out back again and show me how to make the northern lights dance by humming, talk about how God gave us power over everything in the sky, but this was the day that she taught me to scream terror just below the volume of the wind.

Mythology

I can remember well enough being five years old and seeing my father come home from work. I'd run as fast as I could and jump as high as I could to land in the old man's arms, and he'd lift me up and hug me the way that fathers do with their sons, and I can remember what it felt like to be lifted and his face and I can remember all of it except for the emotion, the energy and devotion that must have pushed its way through my body, and has been replaced with the love and respect I have now. It's gone, that feeling, like so many things with it. My brother was born mid-winter in Canada, the day so cold they had to cover his mouth with a cloth so he wouldn't freeze his lungs, and they say that night the northern lights came out to play, and I know myself well enough that I would have cocked my head and thought about the metaphor of it all, and it would have seemed spiritual, but that moment's been scrubbed out of my memory too, and who knows what else is gone, the face of my first childhood best friend and my first crush and so much that was so important to me, gone beyond the salvation of Proust's Madeleine. And I cannot remember the excitement I felt putting on Halloween costumes, although I know that I loved Halloween, or the fear I had of dogs. What's left is the mythology of my life, I suppose, the mythology everyone has deep down beyond the logic of words—the first pear that my father gave to me and no one else, the cat I found in the street and played with silently and never talked about, the summer lightning storm when we lived in Edmonton, me way out on the far end of the backyard, the thunder smashing its way through the sky, but I wasn't afraid because my mother was framed in the back door, calling to me, and that fundamentalist faith I had that as long as she was there even God couldn't reach out his hand and strike me down for the sins written on my childhood soul.

Starbucks on a Saturday Night

The couple in front of me explores each other's faces with fingers, palms and lips, the way that only 15-year-olds can. Then they glance at me to gauge my shock. Their love is defined by the defiance of old men, so the third time they turn their hopeful eyes to me, I glower them into a rebellion of passion that they will never be able to feel just in the same way ever again.

Meditations on a Lightning Storm that Happened in 1894

My great grandfather, who neither I nor my father nor my grandfather ever met, died one night from a single bolt as he tramped across Ohio farmland. Just before the moment, he sighted a light in the upstairs window of his home, and his breath tripped a little in its joy. Inside sat his wife, pregnant with the new child patriarch, the child who died of old age 50 years ago this evening.

Summer 1982

I held back a bit, left my legs mumbling in the grasses just a moment too long, so when the baseball arced out of the sky I could dive head-first into the catch. I waited for the cheers of my friends in a moment that was silent except for the sound of a passing car, except for the sound of the Rain Bird's click.

After the Earthquake

After the earthquake, you call your friends, talk to them, laugh, and a fine sense of holiday spreads all over Los Angeles. Everyone hopes work is canceled for the day.

After the earthquake, you goggle about where you were and what it was like to feel the Earth slipping out from underneath you for a moment.

You talk about that moment of fear and then the elation of still being alive and someone says inevitably she wishes it'd happen again, that it's a free roller coaster and you laugh, and she laughs, and everyone is laughing until you get into your car, and you're alone and you realize that yes, you do wish that it would happen again, that it would happen every day, except you realize that it does, it's just that most earthquakes are tiny, so tiny that we miss them, but the ground beneath us is slipping out from under our feet every moment, every every moment.

Up Towards Weaver Lake

On the way to Weaver Lake, on the long trail that keeps going up and up and up, you get to the place where the mosquitoes are snapping, and you wish you could stop because the sweat is pouring out now, coming off your chest in thin sheets, and that's what's bringing mosquitoes, of course, sweat is the music of their lives, what makes them dance across your body.

Right there, where all the bugs are chewing you, that's where all those trees have fallen, cracked right in half with once-jagged edges, worn down by the years and wind and dirt. This was the place fifty-three years ago where the ice storm hit first and then two days later, the wind storm and all these trees did their final dance, the dance where they all bowed from the waist like gentlemen in old movies greeting their ladies, except these gentlemen never stood back up, these gentlemen danced to the icy ground and slid a little like Fred Astaire in a final show-stopping move.

All of these fine gentlemen danced their death dance alone, no one to see them but each other also dying, alone—the way every living thing in this world dies—their whole world caving in at once, for them and whatever animals used to live here. The world that had once been a fine grove of gentlemen trees and the society of a certain group of animals was replaced in a season by the insects that chew dead wood and the little animals that eat the insects that chew dead wood and the mosquitoes that feast on the little animals but seem to prefer the music of your sweat.

And now all these years later, you're here and part of the feast of the gentlemen's slow decay. You resent them for dying all at once fifty-three years ago and bringing the slow torture of a million bites, and you move out of the area heading anywhere but here, not thinking about the minor apocalypse or the rebirth or the slow decay that is a new form of apocalypse itself. You're distracted from the thousands of apocalypses happening all the time everywhere all around you, and the rebirths too. Distracted from everything but your own cooling sweat and the biting flies.

Poem about the Pacific Crest Trail that Devolves into a Kind of Sentimentality I'm Not Ashamed of

On the couch last night, I realized that I was never going to hike the Pacific Crest Trail—not the whole thing—and I guess I could add that to my long list of regrets if I had ever wasted time with that kind of list.

There was a time twenty years ago when I dreamed of taking the hike from Canada to Mexico in a three-month journey of silence and self-reflection, swimming into myself and finding the peace that lay in the middle.

What a pretentious ass I was, and what a fool I was to think that peace lay some place inside me when it was sitting right there the whole time on the couch in that space beside you.

Sequoia National Park, 1987

The first time I missed church on purpose, I was backpacking by myself, had told Mom and Dad I would drive down to the local church and look God straight in the Eucharist and talk to him.

The first time I missed church on purpose, I spent the afternoon under redwood trees, teenage-poor and arguing with my phantom parents about God and the nation and backing up points with Friedrich Nietzsche and Karl Marx.

The parents of my imagination walked the forest paths with me. At first, they yelled but eventually they were quieted by the logic and purity of my arguments. They listened and paused on our walk to ask questions. They gazed upwards as if to see the blue of the sky for the first time in their lives. Eventually they were silent. My father smiled at a secret joke and shook his head slowly at himself.

The first time I missed church on purpose, I waited until my daydream parents walked away, and then I leaned back and talked directly to God. I asked him all those things I had been dying to ask him all my life, and I waited a full mass hour to hear if he would respond.

San Dimas, 1987

In cross country practice, we had the strange ritual of wrapping shirts around our heads to stop the worst of the sweat stinging our eyes, and we'd arrange our course so we'd be able to sprint in a burst of masculinity past the girls' locker room just as cheerleading let out.

We twenty young men without an ounce of fat, thinking that this pulsating run was what manhood was, that this flesh browning in the smog-alert afternoon was what we'd do every day and all the time when we left high school for the real life outside.

Afterwards I Stayed Outside for an Hour Before They Made Me Come In

I must have been eleven, or maybe I was twelve, the first time I noticed a satellite. It was the first really warm day of summer in 1982, or maybe it was 1983, when the wind coming off the desert had blown the smog out of L.A. and the street lights seemed to glare less than usual, and that satellite crossed Orion, the one constellation I knew, until it got lost behind the orange tree in my parents' backyard.

By the time I'd climbed on top of the garage to see it again, it had vanished, and I stood staring at each star individually—squinting at each one, comparing all of them to the stars nearby making sure they stayed still—to see if they too would lose their grip on the night and fall away into the sky.

Sometimes at Night, It Falls on Me Still

In 1979, Skylab lost its grip on night and fell to Earth, and no one knew where it would land, but we were all afraid it might rip through the sky like a bomb arcing past the USSR and China and the Son of Sam, and that on some late night, it might burst silently through the clouds until it found the roof under which we lay and that it might crush us as we slept, and we would never even know we died.

I Forgot to Say

Do you remember the day Julian died, and you and I walked the trail up to Strawberry Peak? Do you remember how we stood there on the cliff in the dark of the near-snow day listening to the wind roaring—the millions of ice chips floating in the cloud before us—and how the howling wind sounded like a metaphor? Do you remember how you wandered off away from me a bit, into the trees so that your silhouette became watery and loose, and you shouted something I couldn't hear over God using figures of speech?

    I shouted something back that you couldn't hear, and you asked me later what I had said. I kissed you instead, kissed you silent, and you forgot to ask me again, and I forgot to tell you. My darling, it was just what you would expect me to shout over God shrieking bitterness on that kind of day. What else could there ever be, after all, to say?

In Praise of Dogs Who Howl at the Moon

Some nights, everything on Earth is loose, and you feel yourself slipping off gravity's mooring, slipping off into the night, feel the moon's going to grab you and pull you out into space and slingshot you past Mars and Jupiter out to where Pluto and all the rest of the solar system's lost children live, out where you will never see your wife laugh the way she laughs at your jokes when you've been gone a week and you're finally home, laugh with the wild joy of a bear waking up after months of sleep—on those nights you want to grab onto something wedged deep and tight as a tick in a furry ear and scream your complaints at the moon as the dogs howl and the bears roar and everyone shouts together—you want to yell that no one belongs out there in the cold with Pluto, that we belong here where summer love is and anyone who loves and howls is one of Earth's favorite children.

The Wind's Will

It's late November 1982, probably Thanksgiving, but maybe the weekend before, and Dad has taken us out to the desert to fire off my brother's rocket. The rain's coming soon, and the clouds somersault above us.

It's hard to tell how high they are without the reference of a plane or a skyscraper. They could be giants, 20,000 feet above us or only 100 feet up. Mark fires off his rocket, and it goes through a couple of model rocket stages, and then just about when it's going to burst into the final explosion that pushes out the parachute, it's sucked up into the cloud.

The wind's going too hard, so we don't hear the popping last explosion, the final stage of the engine's life, but we stare at the cloud's belly—waiting for the toy to come out the bottom.

The wind bullies the clouds for a good five minutes before we give up, me caught in a wish that I had been the one who'd been pulled up and out of this world into the endless dark gray of midday purgatory.

Edgar Degas's *Waiting*

The little girl and an older woman, obviously her handler, sit on the bench the way two construction workers might before a shift, and why shouldn't they? They're both working people. The little ballerina bends over and is either rubbing pain out of a swollen ankle or adjusting the strap of her slipper, and the woman dressed in mourning black seems to be lost in the kind of thought that adults have when they realize their lives have become just this, just ferrying kids here and there.

I know how that little girl feels not because of some extra helping of empathy. It's just that in my last life, I was her. That day my mother (yes, the woman all in black) let me know what was what. She told me that as hard as this dancing all day was, as bad as it was that I was working full-time at the age of thirteen, it was still better than what was coming, so I'd better stop complaining. Life could be hard on women in Paris, and besides, since my father had died, someone had to pay the bills. That was the day I realized on my own—without anyone telling me—that someday I would sell my body to someone or many someones and the point of all this dancing and mincing and prancing was to whet the appetite, so my mother could get a better price for me.

The thing is, I know how the mother feels too because two lives ago, I was her, and when I told my daughter to shape up, I knew she was smart enough to know what was really happening. And when the show started, and she went on stage, and I could hear all those children before all those men as a sort of dancing menu, I didn't weep for her. I sat thinking about the lie I'd kept up her whole life, about the man who was supposed to be her father, a soldier who'd loved her and me and had given his life for France.

The Sound of an Airplane

The other day, I figured out why I always use the highest locker in the gym. In my high school, only seniors were allowed to use top lockers, and it was a dubious privilege I hungered for through three years.

It's the same with driving. When I come up on a sharp turn, I generally lean into it, no doubt a result of having ridden a motorcycle until I was nearly thirty.

I wish I understood the rest, though. Like why do I feel a little nervous before mowing the lawn? Why am I so uncomfortable in a casino, and why is it that the sound of an airplane always reminds me of a pick-up football game I played twenty-five years ago on a hot Los Angeles afternoon with five guys I never saw before and never saw again?

The Art of Merging

He's been on the road five hours after taking it from his boss all day, when a big white truck cuts into his space on the freeway. He lets it all go at once: the job he didn't want, the miscarriage, the wife he betrayed, his brother's addictions, everything in one long sentence of hatred, and the truck takes his sentence and his sins, and it hauls them away forever like that beautiful goat wandering the Sinai.

The Art of Falling

On the freeway overpasses, on a motorcycle, you sit four feet off the ground, and the guardrails are two feet high, and when traffic is moving, you lean into those turns the way that you lean into any turn, falling towards the ground a bit to keep yourself upright, pushing yourself despite yourself towards the void between you and the people below who could be your final breathless audience.

The Car Breaks Down on the 99 Up Near Fresno

And I suppose, after the repair shops tell me to come back in a couple of days, that I could check out the local sites, the national forests, the beautiful farmland, the rivers I've never seen, the restaurants, the college I've always admired, whatever culture they have here or just walk and walk and walk as I do in most cities, and I suppose that since I've never been here every moment would be a kind of adventure. Even if the world doesn't laud Fresno as it does Paris, which just means it's there for me to explore without the burden of tourism or expectation. I will not be fooled into going to its tourist traps, Fresno's version of the Eiffel Tower, Arch of Triumph, Notre Dame, and I will see the real Fresno in a way that most people never see the real Paris. I suppose that this could be a spiritual and emotional awakening for me, except that I decide to go the other way and sleep. It's the first day of the vacation, after all, and the year catches up to me, one of the best and worst years of my life. All of that washes through me and knocks me on my back for the three days of repair, and I miss what is possibly the jewel of the West, but I find myself again among the reeds and whispers of my dreams.

Waking Up on Highway 99

I wake up somewhere in the middle of the vineyards of California's Great Central Valley, but I might as well be looking out on one of France's famed wine and cheese regions. The two places become a blur for me, but what's the difference after all? Van Gogh might have just as well painted this farmland and found himself just as inspired and lost and disappointed as he was after burying himself in the romantic dream of the old country.

Tuesday and You're Feeling Green

Tuesday slips in like a sheaf of paper stuck in a bookcase between a couple of your books, big books about big things that happen on big days like Fridays, Saturdays, and Sundays—days when you do things like get married and graduate and have parties where you find out you never loved your spouse in the first place and you eat away your pain in big Sunday dinners, but the only big things that happen on Tuesday are the things you can't control like births and falling in love and meeting the people who will be your friends forever and will never betray you even on a Saturday even at a big party where all your old friends from college are invited, even the people you didn't like all that much but your spouse always seemed to adore.

Sitting in My Father's House on a Summer Afternoon While He Is Away

Los Angeles shimmers itself sleepy, and I sit in your living room air conditioning watching the backyard in the silence of your house waiting for the phone call that will come when the doctor is done with you. Outside, the bird feeder you set up a month ago sways back and forth with the rhythmic attack of jays, and the tree that gave you blood poisoning thirty years ago drops an orange. If you were here, you'd walk outside and pick it up, but it's just me, and I like that single blotch of new color that highlights the perfection of your back lawn.

The Late-August Weather Report in Los Angeles

After the fires have been going for a week or so above Los Angeles, the wind shifts and the ash cloud blows out over your house, and it all starts to come down like warm snow, the way you imagined it did in 1980 when Mt. St. Helens cratered, and you wondered then why anyone cared when every night after the news, your parents talked about how the Soviets were going to end everything, how you lived far enough out of town that the first blast wasn't going to kill you but that you'd go slowly in the ashy winter that followed and that the water would be choked and cows would die out in the fields and the whole Earth, all of it, was going to look like Sodom and that you were just going to be one of its least favorite citizens waiting for the warm snow to turn cold and the sun to switch off and your dog to die and your parents to die and then you would die.

You think about how you felt like you could barely breathe all those years, and how you still have a hard time, and now when you look up at the sky and the sun is changing color because of that fire in the foothills, you wonder how much longer you have, that even if the big apocalypse is becoming less and less likely, you have your own horsemen coming.

You look out your front window to see kids staring up into the smoke and ash and laughing about it the way that kids in other parts of the country laugh about snow, and the day is so hot and dirty that everyone is sweating and the dirt in the air becomes mud on their necks and the kids are wearing shorts and dancing their dance in the heat snow, throwing their arms up wildly when they jump, screaming in joyful screams in a kind of dance of Revelation and you think to yourself that this is what the end probably looks like.

Acknowledgements

"The Green of Sunset" was published in Silver Birch Press's *The Green Anthology*; "The Butterfly Effect" was published by *A Few Lines Magazine*; "Poem to the Child Who Was Almost My Son" was published originally as "Poem to the Child Whom I Almost Adopted," along with "Thinking of Wilfred Owen," "Apology to Madeline" and "A Man Stepping into a River," in *Serving House Journal*; "Prince Toto, Despot of the Ant Nation" was published in *Carnival Literary Magazine*; "Building Los Angeles" was published in *Seventh Quarry*; "My Second Self" was published in *Cease Cows*; "God Save the Queen" was published in *Askew*; "The Wages of Cynicism" was published in *In Somnis Veritas*; "Café London" was published in Bank Heavy Press' *Robo Book*; "Meditations on a Lightning Storm that Happened in 1894" was published in *Synesthesia*; "Edgar Degas's *Waiting*" was published in *The Interpreter's House*; "The Art of Merging" was published in *Nerve Cowboy*; "The Art of Falling" was published in *Borderlines*; "Afterwards I Stayed Outside for an Hour Before They Made Me Come In" and "In Praise of Dogs Who Howl at the Moon" were published in Silver Birch Press's *Summer Anthology*; "Parley with the Barbarians," "Edmonton, Summer 1974," "Sequoia National Park, 1987," "Afterwards I Stayed Outside for an Hour Before They Made Me Come Back In," "Sometimes at Night, It Falls on Me Still," "I Forgot to Say," "In Praise of Dogs Who Howl at the Moon," "After the Earthquake," and "The Late-August Weather Report in Los Angeles" were published in *Re)verb*; and "A Man Stepping into a River," "Sequoia National Park, 1987," "San Dimas 1987," "Summer 1982," "The Trail to Bearpaw Meadow, Sequoia National Park, 1978," "The Trail to Bearpaw Meadow, Sequoia National Park, 1985," "The Trail to Bearpaw Meadow, Sequoia National Park, 2005," "Starbucks on a Saturday Night," "Meditations on a Lightning Storm that Happened in 1894," "God Save the Queen," "Stopping at a Target in New York," and "Lightning Storm" were published in *12 Pieces of Silver* from Silverbirch Press.

About the Author

John Brantingham is the author of hundreds of poems, stories and essays published in magazines in the United States and United Kingdom. His books include *Mann of War*, a crime novel, *Let Us All Pray Now to Our Own Strange Gods*, a short story collection, *The Gift of Form*, an instruction guide for beginning formal poetry, and *East of Los Angeles*, a poetry collection. He teaches English at Mt. San Antonio College in Walnut, California and lives in Seal Beach with his wife Annie and dog, Archie Goodboy. Check out his blogs, "John Brantingham" and "Exercising While Reading Rex Stout: The Fitness Hunt," and friend him on Facebook, which he updates obsessively.

Patrons

Moon Tide Press would like to thank the following people for their support in helping us to publish the finest poetry from the Southern California region. To sign up, visit www.moontidepress.com or send an email to publisher@moontidepress.com.

Gloria Avena
Michael Kramer
Lee Mallory
Robert and Michele Miller
Gabriella Miotto
Peter and Ligaya Srisavasdi
Rachanee Srisavasdi

Our thanks as well to the following institutions for their ongoing support:

Orange Lutheran High School
University of California, Irvine
University of California, Santa Barbara

Also Available from Moon Tide Press

Lost American Nights: Lyrics & Poems, Michael Ubaldini (2006)
Tide Pools: An Anthology of Orange County Poetry (2006)
Sleepyhead Assassins, Mindy Nettifee (2006)
A Thin Strand of Lights, Ricki Mandeville (2006)
Kindness from a Dark God, Ben Trigg (2007)
Carving in Bone: An Anthology of Orange County Poetry (2007)
A Wild Region, Kate Buckley (2008)
In the Heaven of Never Before, Carine Topal (2008)
Now and Then, Lee Mallory (2009)
Pop Art: An Anthology of Southern California Poetry (2010)
What We Ache For, Eric Morago (2010)
One World, Gail Newman (2011)
Hopeless Cases, Michael Kramer (2011)
I Was Building Up to Something, Susan Davis (2011)
In the Lake of Your Bones, Peggy Dobreer (2012)
Straws and Shadows, Irena Praitis (2012)
Cosmos: An Anthology of Southern California Poetry (2012)
The Silence of Doorways, Sharon Venezio (2013)
The Savagery of Bone, Timothy Matthew Perez (2013)

www.ingramcontent.com/pod-product-compliance
Lightning Source LLC
Chambersburg PA
CBHW031206090426
42736CB00009B/803